Christmas 2019

This book belongs to:

Lucy May Roscup

_____

Dear Lucy,

When I was in Kindergarten, I checked
Danny and The Dinosaur out of the library.
When your mom was in Kindergarten - she
checked out the same book. It was really
neat because my name was on the card,
And now I am giving you all the stories. We
hope you love them. We love you.

Aunt Linda, Uncle Jon, Tully & Eve

The DANNY AND THE DINOSAUR

Storybook Collection

Syd Hoff

HARPER
An Imprint of HarperCollinsPublishers

TABLE OF CONTENTS

One day Danny went

to the museum.

He wanted to see what was inside.

He saw Indians.

He saw bears.

He saw Eskimos.

He saw guns.

He saw swords.

And he saw . . .

11

DINOSAURS!

Danny loved dinosaurs.

He wished he had one.

"I'm sorry they are not real,"
said Danny.
"It would be nice
to play with a dinosaur."

14

"And I think it would be nice
to play with you,"
said a voice.
"Can you?" said Danny.

15

"Yes," said the dinosaur.

"Oh, good," said Danny.

"What can we do?"

"I can take you for a ride,"

said the dinosaur.

He put his head down

so Danny could

get on him.

"Let's go!" said Danny.

A policeman stared at them.

He had never seen a dinosaur stop

for a red light.

The dinosaur was so tall

Danny had to hold up

the ropes for him.

"Look out!" said Danny.

"Bow wow!" said a dog.

"He thinks you are a car," said Danny.

"Go away, dog. We are not a car."

"I can make a noise like a car,"

said the dinosaur.

"Honk! Honk! Honk!"

"What big rocks,"

said the dinosaur.

"They are not rocks," said Danny.

"They are buildings."

"I love to climb,"

said the dinosaur.

"Down, boy!" said Danny.

The dinosaur had to be very careful
not to knock over houses or stores
with his long tail.

Some people were
waiting for a bus.
They rode on the
dinosaur's tail instead.

"All who want
to cross the street
may walk on my back,"
said the dinosaur.

"It's very nice of you to help me
with my bundles," said a lady.

Danny and the dinosaur went

all over town and had lots of fun.

"It's good to take

an hour or two off

after a hundred million years,"

said the dinosaur.

They even looked at

the ball game.

"Hit the ball,"

said Danny.

"Hit a home run,"

said the dinosaur.

"I wish we had a boat,"

said Danny.

"Who needs a boat?

I can swim,"

said the dinosaur.

"Toot, toot!"

went the boats.

"Toot, toot!" went Danny

and the dinosaur.

33

"Oh, what lovely green grass!"

said the dinosaur.

"I haven't eaten any of that

for a very long time."

"Wait," said Danny.

"See what it says."

PLEASE KEEP OFF

34

They both had ice cream instead.

"Let's go to the zoo

and see the animals," said Danny.

36

Everybody came running

to see the dinosaur.

Nobody stayed to see
the lions.

Nobody stayed to see

the elephants.

Nobody stayed to see

the monkeys.

And nobody stayed to see

the seals,

giraffes or hippos,

either.

"Please go away
so the animals
will get looked at,"
said the zoo man.

"Let's find my friends,"

said Danny.

"Very well,"

said the dinosaur.

"There they are," said Danny.

"Why, it's Danny

riding on a dinosaur,"

said a child.

"Maybe he'll give us a ride."

"May we have a ride?"

asked the children.

"I'd be delighted,"

said the dinosaur.

"Hold on tight," said Danny.

Around and around

the block ran the dinosaur,

faster and faster and faster.

"This is better than

a merry-go-round,"

the children said.

The dinosaur was

out of breath.

"Teach him tricks,"

said the children.

Danny taught the dinosaur

how to shake hands.

"Can you roll over on your back?"

asked the children.

"That's easy,"

said the dinosaur.

"He's smart," said Danny,

patting the dinosaur.

"Let's play hide and seek,"

said the children.

"How do you play it?"

said the dinosaur.

"We hide and you try

to find us," said Danny.

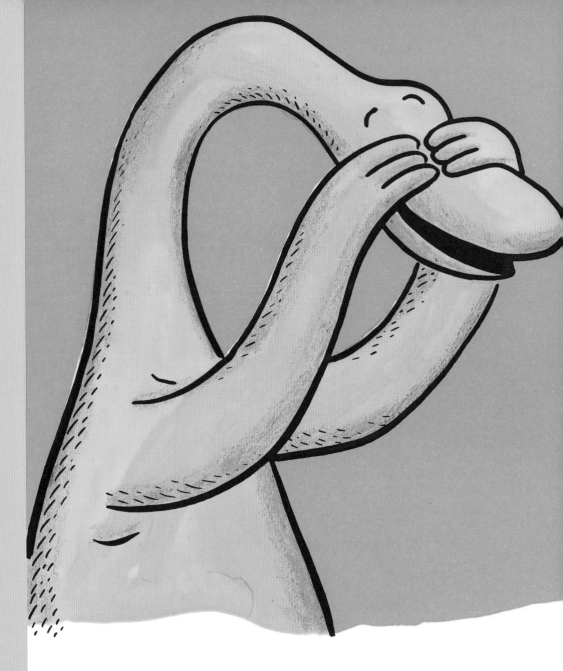

The dinosaur covered

his eyes.

All the children ran
to hide.

The dinosaur

looked and looked

but he couldn't find the children.

"I give up," he said.

Now it was the dinosaur's turn

to hide.

The children covered their eyes.

The dinosaur hid

behind a house.

The children found him.

Brush your teeth every day.

He hid behind a sign.

The children

found him.

He hid behind a big gas tank.

The children found him.

They found him again

and again and again.

"I guess there's no place

for me to hide,"

said the dinosaur.

"Let's make believe

we can't find him," Danny said.

"Where can he be?

Where, oh, where is that dinosaur?

Where did he go?

We give up," said the children.

"Here I am," said the dinosaur.

"The dinosaur wins,"

said the children.

"We couldn't find him.

He fooled us."

"Hurrah for the dinosaur!"

the children cried.

"Hurray! Hurray!"

It got late and

the other children left.

Danny and the dinosaur

were alone.

"Well, goodbye, Danny,"

said the dinosaur.

"Can't you come

and stay with me?"

said Danny.

"We could have fun."

"No," said the dinosaur.

"I've had a good time—

the best I've had

in a hundred million years.

But now I must get back

to the museum.

They need me there."

"Oh," said Danny.

"Well, goodbye."

Danny watched
until the long tail
was out of sight.

Then he went home alone.

"Oh, well," thought Danny,

"we don't have room

for a pet that size, anyway.

But we did have

a wonderful day."

Danny was in a hurry.

He had to see his friend

the dinosaur.

"I'm six years old today,"

said Danny.

"Will you come

to my birthday party?"

"I would be delighted,"

said the dinosaur.

Danny rode the dinosaur

out of the museum.

On the way

they picked up Danny's friends.

"Today I'm a hundred million years

and one day old," said the dinosaur.

"Then it can be your party too!"

said Danny.

The children helped Danny's father

hang up balloons.

"See, I can help too,"

said the dinosaur.

Danny's mother gave out party hats.

"How do I look?"

asked the dinosaur.

"We would like to sing a song,"
said a girl and a boy.

They sang,

and everybody clapped their hands.

"I can sing too," said the dinosaur.

He sang,

and everybody covered their ears.

"Let's play pin the tail

on the donkey," said Danny.

The dinosaur pinned the tail

on himself!

The children sat down to rest.

"Please don't put your feet

on the furniture," said Danny.

The dinosaur put his feet
out the window.

Danny's mother and father

gave each child

a dish of ice cream.

They had to give the dinosaur

more!

"Here comes the birthday cake!"

said the children.

They counted the candles.

"One, two, three, four, five, six."

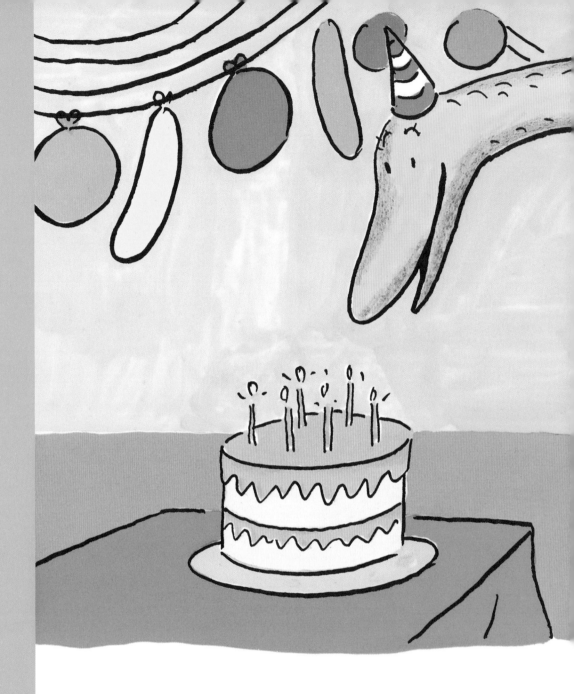

The dinosaur started to eat
the cake.

"Wait!" said Danny.

"First we have to make a wish!"

"I wish we can all be together again
next year," said Danny.
"I wish the same thing,"
said the dinosaur.

They blew out the candles.

"Happy birthday to you!"

everybody sang.

"This is the best birthday party
I have ever had," said Danny.

"Me too," said the dinosaur.

DANNY and the DINOSAUR Go to Camp

Danny went to camp

for the summer.

He took along his friend

the dinosaur.

"Camp is fun.

You will enjoy it," said Danny.

"Thanks. I needed a vacation,"

said the dinosaur.

"Welcome," said the camp owner.

"You're the first dinosaur

we ever had here."

Lana the leader said,

"Let's start with a race.

On your mark, get set, go!"

The dinosaur took a step.

"You win!" shouted Danny.

The children played football.

The dinosaur ran with the ball,

and nobody could stop him.

"Touchdown!" shouted Danny.

Lana took everybody to the lake.

"Here is where we row our boats,"

she said.

The children rowed little boats.

Danny rowed the dinosaur.

It was time for lunch.

"Please pass the ketchup,"

said Danny.

"Of course, just as soon as
I finish this bottle,"
said the dinosaur.

After lunch
everybody wrote letters home.
"Please send me my own ketchup,"
Danny wrote.

"Send me a pizza,"

wrote the dinosaur.

"Now let's go on a hike,"

said Lana,

and everybody followed her.

Then Danny got tired

and climbed on the dinosaur.

"Wait for us!

We're tired too!"

shouted the children.

"Hold tight," said the dinosaur.

The dinosaur even carried Lana!

It got dark.

Everybody sat around the campfire.

Lana gave out toasted marshmallows.

"Here, have all you want,"

she said.

"Thanks, but I don't have room
for more," said Danny.

"I have room,"

said the dinosaur.

It was time for bed.

"I can't wait to get
under the covers,"
said Danny.

"Me too," said the dinosaur.

But the dinosaur's bunk

was too small for him.

He took a pillow
and went outside.

DANNY AND THE DINOSAUR

and the New Puppy

The dinosaur went to the park

to meet his friend Danny.

As he walked up,

he heard Danny say,

"Roll over!"

So the dinosaur rolled over.

THUMP!

"Oops!" said Danny.

"I was talking to my new puppy.

Want to play with us?"

"Let's play!"

said the dinosaur.

Danny threw a stick. "Fetch!"

The puppy came back with the stick.

The dinosaur came back

with a tree.

Danny said, "Sit!"

The puppy sat.

But when the dinosaur sat . . .

CRASH!

He really sat!

"Oops," said the dinosaur.

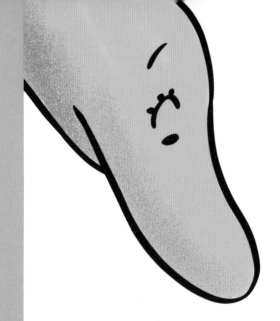

"I'm proud of you both," said Danny.

"Good dog."

He gave the puppy a treat.

"Good dinosaur," said Danny.

He gave the dinosaur lots of treats.

The day was hot.

They went to the pool to cool off.

Splish-splash went the puppy.

SPLISH-SPLASH went the dinosaur.

The friends played at being pirates.

The dinosaur was the pirate ship.

"Ahoy, mateys!" cried Danny.

All the kids climbed on board

while the puppy stood guard.

"Time to dry off," said Danny.

The puppy shook her fur dry.

Shake-shake-shake!

But when the dinosaur tried

to dry himself . . .

Shake-shake-*SPLOOSH!*

everybody got wetter.

The sun set. It was getting late.

"Good-bye, dinosaur," said Danny.

"I wish you could come

home with us."

"Good-bye, Danny," said the dinosaur.

"I wish I could come, too."

The sad dinosaur watched them go.

Then the dinosaur trudged back
to the museum all by himself.

"I wish our day didn't have to end,"

said Danny.

But then he smiled.

Danny had an idea. . . .

"What are you doing here?"

asked the dinosaur.

"Time for a sleepover!" said Danny.

The friends played some quiet games

and had some snacks.

Then they snuggled up to sleep.

"I love sleepovers," said Danny.

"How about you?"

But the dinosaur said nothing.

The dinosaur was asleep.

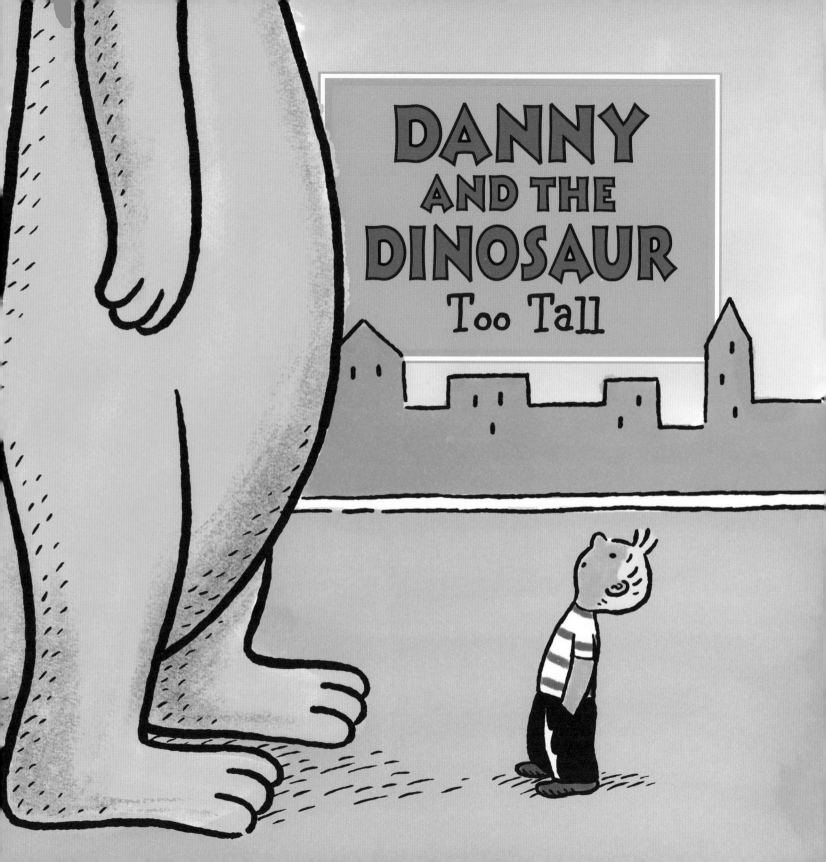

DANNY
AND THE
DINOSAUR
Too Tall

Danny's dinosaur friend was sad.

"What's wrong?" Danny asked.

"It's not easy being different,"

said the dinosaur.

"I don't get it,"

Danny told him.

"Everyone loves dinosaurs."

"And I love being a dinosaur,"
said the dinosaur.
"But that's not my problem."

"Then what's wrong?" said Danny.

The dinosaur sighed.

"I'm just too tall," he said.

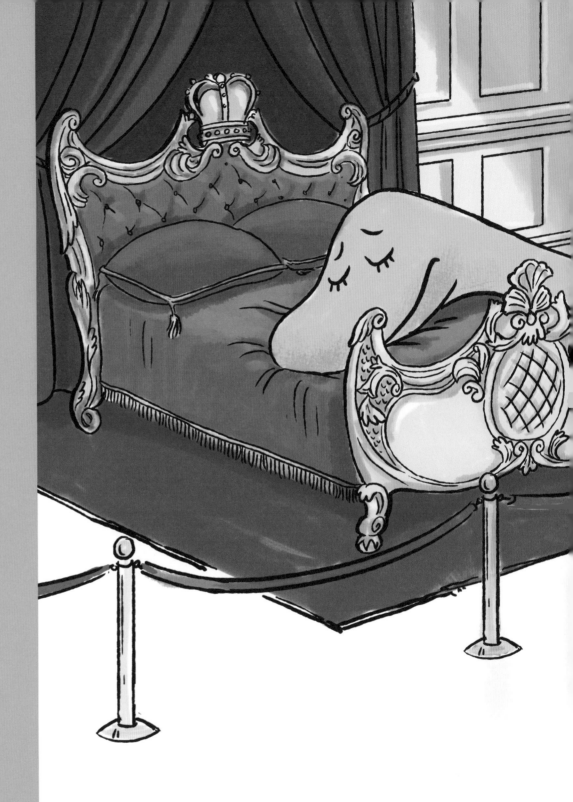

"When I lie in bed,
everything sticks out,"
said the dinosaur.

"When I go through doors,"

said the dinosaur,

"it's no fun at all."

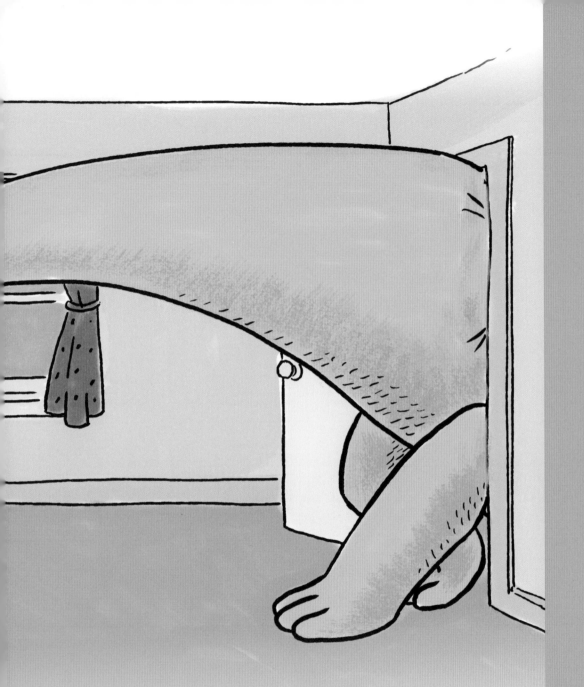

"People ask, 'How's the weather

up there?'" said the dinosaur.

"When I meet new people,
it's hard to say hello."

"Wow," said Danny.

"I had no clue."

The dinosaur nodded.

"Being tall isn't all sunshine
and rainbows," he said.

And the dinosaur hung his head.

"I know what you need," said Danny.

"Come with me!"

And he took the dinosaur for a walk.

"See?" said Danny.

"Elephants are tall, too."

"Not very tall," said the dinosaur.

"Giraffes are tall like you,"

said Danny.

The dinosaur shook his head.

"Nobody's tall like me."

They left the zoo and walked along.

Then the dinosaur saw a man
at his own eye level!

"Wait," he said. "Who's that?"

"Hello," said the dinosaur.

"How's the weather up there?"

"Just fine," said the man.

"I can see for miles."

Danny and the dinosaur

watched the man work,

lifting heavy things.

But then . . .

. . . the wind gusted,
and the crane swayed.
The man was in danger!

"Help him!" someone yelled.

"He can't get down!"

Danny and the dinosaur came closer.

The dinosaur stretched out his neck.

"Hold on to me," he said.

The man grabbed on . . .

. . . and the dinosaur took him
safely to the ground.

"Lucky thing you showed up,"
said the man. "Thank you!"
The dinosaur smiled.
"What is it?" said Danny.

"I've changed my mind,"
said the dinosaur.
"Being tall is great after all."

ISBN 978-0-06-247070-6

Typography by Lori S. Malkin
16 17 18 19 20 SCP 10 9 8 7 6 5 4 3 2 1

First Edition